I was Born 2 Win

CLEVEANN BLACKSTONE

I was Born 2 Win

CLEVEANN BLACKSTONE

Lithonia, GA

© 2022 – Cleveann Blackstone
All rights reserved.

No part of this publication may be reproduced, stored in a retrieval system or transmitted in any form or by any means, electronic, mechanical, photocopying, recording or otherwise, without the expressed written permission of the publisher.

Scripture references are taken from the King James Version of the Holy Bible unless otherwise noted.
Pronouns for referring to the Father, Son and Holy Spirit are capitalized intentionally and the words satan and devil are never capitalized.

I Was Born 2 Win
Publisher:
MEWE, LLC
www.mewellc.com

First Edition
ISBN: 978-1-7360565-3-0

Library of Congress Control Number: 2022902001

Printed in the United States of America.

To my adoptive parents the late Virgil and Selynia Cole Blackstone and to my natural parents Leon and Alene Franks McCall.

To my special friend Annie Rose Hollingsworth Austin who was also adopted. We have remained friends, encouraging each other since Wenonah Elementary School.

To Clarence and Eleanor Lanier Nabors whom I have known over 45 years. Thanks for being there for me and helping me with my girls. May God continue blessing you.

And to the late Nadine Saffold Williams who encouraged me to "Always hold your head up high. Never let the enemy feel they won." I miss you.

To all my family members and friends who have supported me.

Most of all, to my Father which art in Heaven, who gave me the title of this book more than five years ago before I started writing. He has blessed me over and over again. His love encourages me to believe "I Was Born To Win."

TABLE OF CONTENTS

Acknowledgements ix

Preface xi

Chapter 1 – In Christ, We Are Victorious 1

Chapter 2 – Your Daily Confession 7

Chapter 3 – The Prayer that Helped Me 11

Chapter 4 – Your Adversary, the Devil 15

Chapter 5 – Maintaining by Proclaiming 21

Chapter 6 – Unleashing Unwavering Faith 25

Chapter 7 – Why Change? 31

Chapter 8 – Forgetting Things Behind You 35

About the Author 39

Acknowledgements

The late Reverend J. T. Jamar my first Pastor, Bryant Chapel A.M.E. Church, Birmingham, Alabama

The late Reverend John and the late Dorothy Rogers Porter, Sixth Avenue Baptist Church, Birmingham, Alabama

Bishop Donald E. and Gwendolyn Battle, Divine Faith International Church, Jonesboro, Georgia

Pastor Isaiah and Deborah Waddy, St. Paul A.M.E. Church, Atlanta, Georgia

Dr. Cheryl Minter, Pastor of Anointed Word Life Center, Atlanta, Georgia

Bishop Harry Seawright, 9th Episcopal District AME Church

Pastor Damien Littlejohn, Bryant Chapel A.M.E. Church, Birmingham, Alabama

Pastor Jim McCann III, Victory Christian Fellowship, Adamsville, Alabama

Monte A. Horton and Mary Johnson for in depth Bible teaching

Pastor Patricia Anthony, Natchitoches, Louisiana

There are so many who helped me along the road. I can't list all of you but know that I love and appreciate you for your contributions. My passion is helping and giving. I love people. This book is a way of helping someone who needs to get back on track.

Preface

I was born to Leon and Alene Franks McCall on September 22, 1952. When I was still a baby, my neighbors from next door Virgil and Selynia Blackstone fell in love with me and later adopted me. They had only one daughter Lillie Mae Brookins, who lived in Detroit, Michigan. I was at the time one of my four siblings living next door.

My adoptive mother was someone who believed in going to church. She told me that if I could not go to church, I could not go anywhere else. Who wanted to sit at home all day Sunday? Not me. I went to church every Sunday, rain, shine, or snow.

We were members of Bryant Chapel A.M.E. Church in Birmingham, Alabama. I enjoyed church. I was an usher in my smart black skirt and white blouse, I sang in the choir, and later became a Sunday School teacher.

My parents were firm on what they believed in. They may have spared the rod sometimes, but you did what they asked, never talked back and you'd better not get in the way of an adult conversation! Unlike children these days, respect was not a choice; it was a way of living peacefully without being sore. If you didn't speak to the lady on the porch down the street, by the time you got home, a switch might be waiting for you, and you still had to go back down the street to speak.

Even now, I can hear my mother's disciplining voice. I heard it when I was raising my three girls. She would tell me that whatever she said would go in one ear and out the other. But not all of it was lost. There were invaluable lessons as well. I learned from her how to love and help people. I, like everyone else, made mistakes, but I learned from them. Some mistakes took longer to recover from or led to an unpleasant experience to get back on track.

As a child going to Sunday School and Church, I learned a lot from the Bible. I learned even more as ongoing events became more challenging. I learned to be humble and let the Father, Jesus, and the Holy Spirit fight my battles. Believe me, I've had some!

Praise God!

I am always looking for ways to help people.

When I started working for the airline and wanted to minister in Africa, there were eyebrows raised. I explained that not everyone is faced with the opportunity to travel free and I could.

This is how God worked it out for me. I was looking at a preacher on television ministering in Africa with Africans running alongside his car and I said, "God, this should be me over there preaching." Two months later, I received a phone call from a friend, and she said, "Guess what, girl? We are going to Africa to minister!" Immediately, I looked up and thanked God. When we were leaving Africa after ministering, the people were running behind our vehicle.

Want God to do it? Oh yes, He will.

I've made many mistakes in my life, and I know it was only God who brought me out. I had to call upon the name of Jesus every time.

He took my nothing and made me something. He showed me that, no matter what I go through, by His grace and mercy, I can be a winner. He didn't create me to be a failure all my life. He showed me how to turn around and be the person I was created to be. If you're stuck in a rut or heading the wrong way, it's not too late for you either.

God gives everyone free will, that is, the freedom to choose your own way of life. The Bible gives you the guidelines. It's your choice, for good or bad. It is not your parents', your friend's or acquaintance's choice. You choose the life you want to live. I pray it is in line with the Word of God.

This book is to let you know God still has His hands on you.

So, say with me, "I Was Born 2 Win!"

CHAPTER 1

IN CHRIST, WE ARE VICTORIOUS

But thanks be to God, which giveth us victory through our Lord Jesus Christ (1 Corinthians 15:57).

Did you read that? We have victory through Jesus Christ. When we trust and believe in Him, no one can take our victory from us.

> *For God so loved the world that he gave His only begotten Son, that whosoever believeth in him should not perish, but have everlasting life. For God sent not his Son into the world to condemn the world; but that the world through him might be saved* (John 3:16-17).

Whosoever is Anybody. No matter what anyone tells you, you tell them God said "Whosoever."

Whosoever means, "No matter how they criticize you, God said 'whosoever.' No matter how they talk about you, God said 'whosoever.'"

He sent His Son Jesus to enable us to have everlasting life through salvation.

Jesus was sent by God to save the world. All He needs is willing bodies. It's not hard. As you go through your trials and testing (from the devil's temptations), Jesus will be right there to help you, and the Holy Spirit will teach you how to become an overcomer.

I come to tell you… **YOU WERE BORN 2 WIN!**

So, start speaking this, "I Was Born To Win," until you feel it in your spirit. It will put a smile on your face and a spring in your heart.

> *Humble yourselves therefore under the mighty hand of God, that he may exalt you in due time. Casting all your care upon Him; for he careth for you. Be sober, be vigilant; because your adversary the devil, as a roaring lion, walketh about seeking whom he may devour* (I Peter 5:6-8).

People – adults, youth, children of God – let no one persuade you the devil does not exist, or in plain English, there is no devil. I am here to tell you the Word of God says the devil exists, and THAT SETTLES THAT.

This devil is not running around aimlessly. He is intentional. He is stalking, looking, and seeking to steal your joy, your inheritance. But, most of all, he wants to steal The Word of God from your heart and replace it with his evil thoughts and desires.

Guess what? Sometimes we let him in when we do things we shouldn't, just to fit in, just to be popular, to avoid being bullied, or just to prove we're someone we're not. It still doesn't work. We end up worse than before we made these mistakes, and the devil is sitting there laughing at us.

Ya'll know what I am talking about.

You see, the devil is on a mission and his time is running out. Look at all the destruction around us today: school shootings, hate crimes, other killings, stealing and looting, destruction of property ... the list goes on.

This is not God's plan for our lives. These are the signs of the times.

We need to learn more about the people we associate with. Pray and ask God to show you, and have an open eye and ear when He does.

Make use of Technology to help you. You can check out their Facebook page, or Google their names. Do your research? Are they Christian? Where do they attend church? Seek, and with God's help, you will find what you need. When their agenda is revealed to you, don't ignore the signs. You see, we fall so deeply into traps set up by the enemy, and God is constantly telling us to come out.

Most of all, present yourselves as the Christian you profess to be 24-7.

You see, we all know right from wrong; yet sometimes we indulge in wrongdoing and sinful pleasures not caring about the consequences.

We must ask Jesus our Savior to help us get through these temptations.

Jesus is coming back and the devil will finally be defeated. Stay on the winning side.

One of Michael Jackson's songs I love is *Man In The Mirror*. It goes like this, "I'm starting with the man in the mirror. I am asking him to change his ways."

Look deeply into the mirror and, if you don't like what you see, ask Jesus to help you change. He is your only – I said – ONLY source.

Stand your ground against evil.

YOU WERE BORN 2 WIN!

We need to have a personal relationship with the Father, the Son and the Holy Spirit every day of our lives.

Pray More.

Thank God More.

Love God More.

We were not born to be losers. We serve a winning God.

So, let go of the peer pressure, and press into God.

Pray. I hear people all the time saying they don't know how to pray.

You don't need a PhD in prayer; you just need a humble heart to make your request known unto Him. He loves you so much, He bought you at a price – His very life.

I dare you to try Him. He will open doors for you that no man can open and close doors no man can shut.

He is our Lord, Savior, Healer, Deliverer, and Comforter. He is our Light in the darkness.

Praise God, God in Three Persons! O Blessed Trinity!

But thanks be to God, which giveth us the victory through our Lord Jesus Christ. Therefore, my beloved brethren, be ye steadfast, unmoveable, always abounding in the works of the Lord, forasmuch as ye know that your labour is not in vain in the Lord (1 Corinthians 15:57-58).

YOU WERE BORN 2 WIN!

CHAPTER 2

YOUR DAILY CONFESSION

I am a Christian.

I believe in God the Father, Maker of Heaven and earth.

I believe in Jesus Christ, His only begotten Son, my Savior, My Redeemer, My Lord, My Healer.

I believe in the Holy Spirit, who dwells in me, My Comforter, My Teacher.

God in Three Persons, Blessed Trinity!

I am a blessed child of God.

I am the first not the last because He said the last shall be the first.

I am a conqueror.

I can do all things through Christ who strengthens me.

I am an overcomer.

I am a champion not a chump.

I can move mountains with the faith of a mustard seed (Your mountain maybe smoking, drugs, drinking, lying, etc.).

I have been redeemed by the blood of the Lamb.

I know no weapon formed against me shall prosper.

I am a joint heir with Christ.

I WAS BORN 2 WIN!

This book is not written to force you into Christianity. What I love about God is He gives everyone free will, freedom to choose your own way of life. Whatsoever you choose will be your own destiny. He has given us the Bible to live by.

###

I am writing this book to let you know it is not too late to change your destiny.

YOU WERE BORN 2 WIN!

But ye are a chosen generation, a royal priesthood, an holy nation, a peculiar people; that ye should shew forth the praises of him who hath called you out of the darkness into his marvellous light (1 Peter 2:9).

CHAPTER 3

THE PRAYER THAT HELPED ME

Giving honor to my Father who is in Heaven, to my Lord and Savior Jesus Christ and to the Holy Spirit my Comforter, I submit my life to You.

Forgive me, Lord, for all of my sins both known and unknown.

Lord I have Your love in my heart, but I need Your guidance. Fix me, Lord Jesus. I know with You I can be made whole.

I confess You are my Lord and Savior. I believe Jesus died for me, was raised up from the dead and God set Him at His own right hand in the Heavenlies.

Lead me in the direction You would have me to go, so I won't stray from You.

I realize now I have not been the person I should have been, but I know I need to change. I have been broken, but now I know I was born to be a winner in Your eyes.

The world is trying to keep people from being sincere in their worship and trying to sway everyone their way. But God, who has all power, will have the last word.

Help me, O God, to be a living example of Your love which would change hearts.

Give me the holy boldness to speak Your words to uplift myself as well as others.

Father, I don't have enough words to give You all the praise You deserve, but what I have I give to You.

Fix me, Jesus. Make my crooked places straight. Help me to keep on the whole armor of God so that I may withstand the fiery darts of the enemy and those who follow the evil one. Let no corrupt communication come out of my mouth. Guide my tongue. I know man alone cannot tame the tongue, but with prayer, You can. With You all things are possible.

God, there is none like You.

I will sing of the goodness of Jesus and how He saved my soul and made me whole.

Thank You, Lord, for this day that You have made.

I WAS BORN 2 WIN!

CHAPTER 4

YOUR ADVERSARY, THE DEVIL

Humble yourselves therefore under the mighty hand of God, that he may exalt you in due time: casting all your care upon him; for he careth for you.

Be sober, be vigilant; because your adversary the devil, as a roaring lion, walketh about seeking whom he may devour (1 Peter 5:6-8).

We have discussed how the devil intentionally seeks to steal your joy, your inheritance, and most of all, the word of God in your heart. Knowing his time is short, he is working overtime to increase his deception, so that he will have control over our lives.

Yes, he is a deceiver and sneaks on us unawares. It's time to wake up and realize we need to develop a closer relationship with our Creator God. Then you will learn to listen to His voice and not the voice of a stranger (see John 10:4-5).

Without a shadow of a doubt, Jesus is coming back soon. All the signs given by Jesus point to it (see Matthew 24 and Luke 21). The devil will be finally defeated and ultimately cast into the lake of fire (see Revelation 20:10). The Trinity: God the Father, God the Son, and God the Holy Spirit, will reign in heaven and on earth forever. Satan will only lead you to hell and the lake of fire.

Satan is already a defeated foe. Then what will you do??? You have followed a leader that was doomed the minute he stepped out of God's grace, one who has used his clever maneuvering to convince you he is higher and more powerful than God. That is his motive. The truth is he was cast out of heaven a long time ago.

How art thou fallen from heaven, O Lucifer, son of the morning! how art thou cut down to the ground, which didst weaken the nations?

For thou hast said in thine heart, I will ascend into heaven, I will exalt my throne above the stars of God: I will sit also upon the mount of the congregation, in the sides of the north:

I will ascend above the heights of the clouds; I will be like the most High (Isaiah 14:12-14).

Although satan knows he has already been defeated, he still tries to exalt his throne higher than God's in the minds of unbelievers. They do this when they give him a chance to deceive them.

But make no mistake: he is your adversary who is after your soul. He gives you false hope, making you feel like you are on top of the world, yet deceiving you and keeping you from receiving the inheritance that God has for you.

You were Born 2 Win. Satan knows this. He also knows his time is running out and this is why he is walking around trying to enlist as many candidates as he can for his army.

If he actually believes he can defeat the "King of Kings," the "Lord of Lords," then he has really lost his mind. Did you know, all Jesus has to do is speak a word, and the devil and his cohorts will be cast in chains. But that will eventually be his fate at the end of time.

> *Yet thou shalt be brought down to hell, to the sides of the pit. They that see thee shall narrowly look upon thee, and consider thee, saying, Is this the man that made the earth to tremble, that did shake kingdoms…* (Isaiah 14:15-16).

The nations will see this and wonder how they could have followed such a person.

This is not who you want to follow, no matter how he entices you with things that look good. Believe me, they are not. They are just seductions that will lead you to evil.

Be a winner. Move over to the winning circle, to a God who loves you from the heart. Humble yourself under the mighty hand of God.

Pray for your own deliverance and the deliverance of your family and nation. Prayer changes things. Prayer will move mountains in your life. Prayer will clear your path for the blessings of God to flourish in your life. When you look in the mirror, you will see a glow only God can give, and you will know you are a winner. The devil will have lost his place in your life.

But standing against the devil is a process. It starts by admitting your errors.

The devil will definitely try to win you back; this is why you must resist him.

Submit yourselves therefore to God. Resist the devil, and he will flee from you (James 4:7).

You cannot face this road by yourself. The good thing is, God is with you 24/7. Watch how He will exalt you. Surrender all to Him.

Humble yourselves therefore under the mighty hand of God, that he may exalt you in due time: Casting all your care upon him; for he careth for you (1 Peter 5:6-7).

God loves you and wants the best for you. Stay connected.

If you do this, the devil will fail in keeping you from your blessings, the love of God the Father, the salvation of Jesus Christ and the joy of having a Comforter. Praise God!

You can shout now. You know how to defeat the devil. He is powerless when it comes to you. He cannot sift you like wheat. God's hedge of protection surrounds you. Lift up your head. You were BORN 2 WIN!

Once your mind is made up to follow Jesus, no weapon formed against you will prosper (see Isaiah 54:17). You have just stepped into the realm of divine protection.

Again, the devil will try you, but you are more than a conqueror. You have the necessary tools to cast out evil spirits. You have the power of prayer and the authority to use the mighty name of Jesus (see Luke 10:19).

This should put a shout in your mouth and blessed assurance in your heart.

God is a winner. Satan is definitely a loser. God is original. Satan is a copycat. Stay on the winning side.

YOU WERE BORN 2 WIN!

CHAPTER 5

MAINTAINING BY PROCLAIMING

But thanks be to God which giveth us the victory through our Lord Jesus Christ. Therefore, my beloved brethren, be ye steadfast, unmoveable, always abounding in the work of the Lord, forasmuch as ye know that your labour is not in vain in the Lord. (I Corinthians 15:57-58)

In order to maintain your dedication to Christ, you must know your position in Christ. This comes from your relationship with Christ. Are you really ready to give your life to Christ? You must be steadfast, firmly loyal and constantly unwavering, certain that the God life is what you want. Make sure you want to be heaven bound and not hell bound.

You can't say one thing, and then do another if it is not pleasing to God. You must stay on course. Know what you want and go ahead with it.

Maintaining your walk with Christ is speaking and believing the right things. The more you speak about the goodness of God and read His Word (the Bible), the more knowledge you will pour into your spirit. Righteousness will become your friend because it will warn you when you approach the wrong path.

Three things must be included in your prayers:

1. Daily confession that Jesus Christ is the Lord of your life

2. Asking for forgiveness for sins known and unknown

3. Praying in the Holy Spirit for holiness, boldness and strength

If you need help, you can have a BYOB Party (Bring Your Own Bible). Invite friends and study the Bible together. This is a very uncaring world. There are a lot of people who believe in Jesus, but are not Christ-like in their attitude towards others. Having prayer warriors or prayer partners will help them and you build your faith walk.

YOU WERE BORN 2 WIN!

CHAPTER 6

UNLEASHING UNWAVERING FAITH

Now faith is the substance of things hoped for, the evidence of things not seen (Hebrews 11:1).

Having faith, means we are confident of what we hope for and convinced that what we do not see with the naked eye still exists.

How do we get this faith?

So then faith cometh by hearing and hearing by the Word of God (Romans 10:17).

Hearing comes from reading and meditating on the Word, listening to preachers in Church, on the radio, television, and even on Facebook.

Unwavering faith is consistent faith.

It's standing firm on what the word of God says.

It means not changing your thought pattern.

It encourages you to keep your eyes on the prize, your full salvation when you meet Jesus face to face.

Some people will speak to you with a smile one minute and then turn their backs on you the next. Some will pray only when they need something from the Father, Jesus, or the Holy Spirit. When they get what they want, they do not call on them until they need something else. This is unstable or wavering faith.

God is not a water fountain you can turn on when you need something, and turn off when you don't.

Let's look in the book of Daniel, Chapter 3:1-6:

Nebuchadnezzar the King made an image of Gold, whose height was three score cubit, and breadth thereof six cubits; he set it up in the plains of Dura, in the province of Babylon (verse 1).

This statue was a visible sign to all of the King's great exploits. Nebuchadnezzar ordered every person in his kingdom to bow down and worship the golden image when they heard certain music playing. Anyone refusing to bow down would be burned in the fiery furnace in the same hour.

Like right then. You would be burned. No bow, no life. WOW!

King Nebuchadnezzar had three intelligent Hebrew boys serving him in the palace. Their Hebrew names were changed from Hananiah, Mishael, and Asariah to Shadrach, Meshach, and Abednego. Daniel had requested they be set over the affairs of the province of Babylon. I told you they were intelligent and also brave.

Well, when King Nebuchadnezzar learned these Hebrew boys would not bow down to his golden image at the sound of his special music, he was furious. Of course, he commanded them to be brought to him.

When they arrived, He commanded them to bow down and worship the golden image at the sound of the music, or else they would be cast into the fiery furnace. He challenged them asking what God could deliver them out of his hands.

Now look closely at how the three young men answered him:

> *O King Nebuchadnezzar we are not careful to answer thee in this matter. If it be so, our God whom we serve is able to deliver us from the burning fiery furnace, and he will deliver us out of thine hand, O king. But if not, be it known unto thee, O king, that we will not serve thy gods, nor worship the golden image which thou hast set up* (Daniel 3:16-18).

That's Unwavering Faith.

The King was so full of fury, he ordered the furnace to be heated up seven times hotter. (Didn't want to be outdone.) Sounds like some folks you know!!!

It was so hot it slew the men who took Shadrach, Meshach, and Abednego to the furnace. But as for the three men, they could be seen walking in the midst of the fiery flames.

The King was astounded.

> *Did we not cast three men bound into the midst of the fire... Lo, I see four men loose, walking in the midst of the fire, and they have no hurt; and the form of the fourth is like the Son of God"* (verses 24, 25).

How could he say the fourth looked like the Son of God? Jesus hadn't yet come in the flesh. It lets you know the Son of God was already performing miracles before He came in the flesh.

It's like Noah's Faith:

It rained forty days and forty nights, but Noah and family were safe in the ark.

In this episode we see:

Faith Demonstrated – When they wouldn't bow down.

Faith Challenged – When the furnace was heated up seven times hotter.

Faith Vindicated – When the fourth Person Jesus showed up in their midst.

Unwavering Faith – When they trusted God with their most prized possession, their very lives.

Seeing those things taken care of in your life through spiritual eyes rather than natural eyes is giving substance to faith (see Hebrews 12:1).

Knowing who the author and finisher of your faith is gives you endurance to run your race (see Hebrews 12:2).

Faith works patience (see James 1:3).

Faith is knowing there is one who is able is able to do exceedingly and abundantly above all you could ever ask or think (see Ephesians 3:20).

Faith in delighting yourself in the Lord is the only way that God will give you the desires of your heart (see Psalm 37:4).

Without faith it is impossible to please Him (see Hebrews 11:6).

Hallelujah!

Will you accept this unwavering faith?

Can you stand against evil and say YES to God?

Start confessing:

Yes, to Your will, Oh God.

Yes, to Your ways, Oh God.

Yes, Lord.

Yes, Jesus.

Yes, Holy Spirit.

I WAS BORN 2 WIN!

CHAPTER 7

WHY CHANGE?

There is right and there is wrong. There is good and there is evil. There is life and there is death. There is happiness and there is sadness. There is day and there is night. There is light and there is darkness. There is love and there is hate. There is Heaven and there is Hell. None of these can happen to you in the same moment. It has to be one or the other.

Right, good, life, happiness, day, light, love, and Heaven can be illustrated in the Love of God. He is all of these. He is your light in the darkness. He gives you comfort in uncertain times.

When I was a young girl going to church, we had to memorize this psalm:

The LORD is my shepherd; I shall not want.

He maketh me to lie down in green pastures: he leadeth me beside the still waters.

He restoreth my soul: he leadeth me in the path of righteousness for his name's sake,

Yea, though I walk through the valley of the shadow of death, I will fear no evil; for thou art with me; thy rod and thy staff they comfort me.

Thou preparest a table before me in the presence of mine enemies; thou anointest my head with oil; my cup runneth over.

Surely goodness and mercy shall follow me all the days of my life and I will dwell in the house of the LORD for ever (Psalm 23).

Learn this Scripture by heart. Just knowing God has your back when you make that change is really a life changing experience.

You see, we were all faced one time or the other with peer pressure. If you let it, it will rob you of your joy. Memorizing this scripture will help you to overcome any obstacle.

To change, you must have an open door to the gateway of God. You need to continuously talk to God.

Don't Worry About What People Are Going to Say

I lost friends when I changed my life. Later I found out they weren't my friends anyway.

So, don't worry about what people are going to say about your life changes. Stick to your choice. When you stand before God, you will stand alone. Those people will not be with you. You are judged by yourself.

With some people, unless something is their idea, they reject it. Your choice to make Jesus Christ your Lord and Savior is a big step toward redemption.

The devil gets upset and will use your friends against you. But know that your body was made to glorify God.

What? know ye not that your body is the temple of the Holy Ghost which is in you, which ye have of God, and ye are not your own? For ye are bought with a price: therefore glorify God in your body, and in your spirit, which are God's (1 Corinthians 6:19-20).

Reach deep down in your heart and feel the power of the love of Jesus moving. It is as refreshing as a summer breeze. You will feel a sense of freedom. Joy to be in His presence will envelop you.

Always know God loves you and He wants only the best for you. People will try to bring the old you back by trying lead you away from God. Stand firm and see the salvation of God. God has a storehouse full of blessings with your name on it. Don't let anyone take what was designed for you.

I heard a preacher once say, "If you don't want it, I'll take it." I thought about this. "If I am not going to let any rock cry out for me, I am sure not going to let anyone get my blessings."

I want all that God has for me. I can truly say over the years God has really blessed me. Keep praying, keep talking to Him, keep fasting and praying, and reading the Bible. All this will keep your faith moving in the right direction. Block all the negatives and move closer to God.

CHAPTER 8

FORGETTING THINGS BEHIND YOU

So many times we have things in our lives we need forgiveness for, but we are afraid to ask God. He forgives and forgets. But we never forget. We allow the enemy (the devil) to plague us with these things. He keeps reminding us through our thoughts of a person, a family member, or a loved one, and how they hurt us.

But, as we learn more about the Father, the Son, and the Holy Spirit, our faith gets stronger. We learn to bring our burdens before God and know He will embrace us and forgive our sins. He will give us grace to forgive others. We are only one prayer away from a breakthrough. Just open your mouth and call upon Him. Open your mouth and rebuke the devil. Put him in his place with all his cohorts. Surrender your feelings to God and ask Him to help you battle these deceptive thoughts.

Prayer: Father, Lord Jesus, and Holy Spirit, please help me forget those things which are behind me and let me reach for those things which are before me. Let me press more into You. I love You and I know when I call upon the name of Jesus, all demons must leave. Jesus is the name above all names and is a powerful name. Teach me to make this my daily prayer. Amen.

Blessed is the man that walked not in the council of the ungodly, nor sitteth in the seat of the of the scornful.

But his delight is in the Lord; and in His law doth he meditate day and night.

And he shall be like a tree planted by the rivers of waters that bringeth forth his fruit in his season; his leaf also shall not wither, and whatsoever he doeth shall prosper (Psalm 1:1-3).

.Forget those things which are behind you. With all that is going on in this world, just focus on Jesus.

Meditate on His word day and night. He is waiting on you.

YOU ARE DEFINITELY BORN TO WIN!

Remember, it's not too late. He will meet you right where you are. Just call on the name of Jesus. Be sincere. Let it come from your heart and you will feel His heart.

Come to Him as a Child. He loves all His children and wants the best for them.

You will learn how to laugh at the attacks of the enemy because God, Jesus, and the Holy Spirit have got your back. The enemy will soon learn not to cross your path. He will try to use people around you, but you are aware of that, too, so you can pray for guidance.

Watch the joy you once had come back to your life. Watch the relief from pressure in your everyday life. People will look at you and want that same joy. Tell them how you got it. Testify.

I pray this book has helped you as the Lord has helped me.

I have had some challenges in my life but, as I think back and look around, He has truly blessed me.

I pray for your blessing. Be true to God and yourself. He knows all and sees all.

Remember, my friend…

YOU WERE BORN 2 WIN!

About the Author

Cleveann Blackstone is a licensed Minister of the Gospel. She presently attends Bryant Chapel A.M.E. Church, Birmingham, Alabama and serves as President of Greater Titusville Civitan Club (2021-2022).

After graduation from Wenonah High School and Lawson State Community College in Birmingham, Alabama, Cleveann attended Clark College, and Atlanta Area Technical School. She later attended Divine Faith School of Ministry, and was licensed by Dr. Cheryl Minter, Pastor of Anointed Word Life Center.

Cleveann attended two of Kenneth Hagin's Ministry Conferences in Tulsa, Oklahoma and was privileged to have ministered in the United States as well as in Nakuru, Kenya, and Ochoa Rios, Jamaica.

Cleveann's experience in sales for over 30 years has given her the opportunity to listen and talk to strangers. Some shared joy and some shared sadness. It is her ardent prayer that this book will bring joy to many.

She is blessed to be the mother of three beautiful young ladies: twins, Andrea D. Nabors and Undrea D. Matthis, and Shola G. Nabors, together with nine grandchildren and one great-grandson.

www.ingramcontent.com/pod-product-compliance
Lightning Source LLC
Chambersburg PA
CBHW030916080526
44589CB00010B/339